GREAT TALES FROM LONG AGO

THESEUS AND THE MINOTAUR

Retold by Catherine Storr
Illustrated by Ivan Lapper

Methuen Children's Books

in association with Belitha Press Ltd.

Note: The source for the story is *The Greek Myths* by Robert Graves.

CS

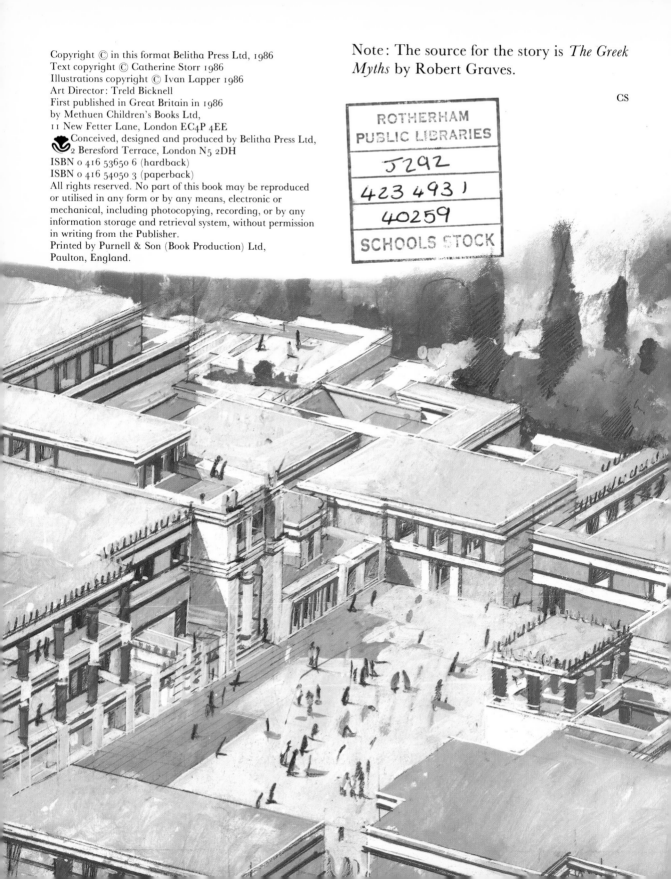

LONG AGO, ON THE ISLAND OF CRETE,
there lived a powerful King, called Minos.
He had a beautiful wife
and a lovely daughter, called Ariadne.
He had a splendid palace
between the mountains and the sea.
But the splendid palace held a terrible secret.

Minos' wife had given birth to a monster.
This monster had the body of a man, and the head of a bull.
It was wild and fierce and it ate human flesh.
Minos was ashamed and wanted to hide the monster.
A clever craftsman, called Daedelus,
built a hiding place underneath the palace,
where the monster could be kept.
This hiding place had many passages and turnings.
No one who did not know the secret
could find his way out.
This was the Labyrinth, or maze.

FAR AWAY FROM THE ISLAND OF CRETE,
on the other side of the Aegean Sea,
stood the proud city of Athens.
Once in every nine years, the people of Athens
were forced to send to King Minos
seven young men and seven young women.
After they had sailed for Crete,
these men and women were never seen again.
People said that when they reached Crete,
they were sacrificed to some horrible monster.

AEGEUS, THE KING OF ATHENS,
had a son, Theseus.
One day, Theseus asked his father
"Why are so many people in the city
anxious and sad and weeping today?
Is some danger threatening us?
Tell me, and I will go out and fight
our enemy."
His father answered,
"There is nothing you can do,
my brave son. It is now nine years
since we last sent our boys and girls
across the sea to King Minos.
Tomorrow the lots will be cast
to discover which families in Athens
are to lose their sons and daughters."

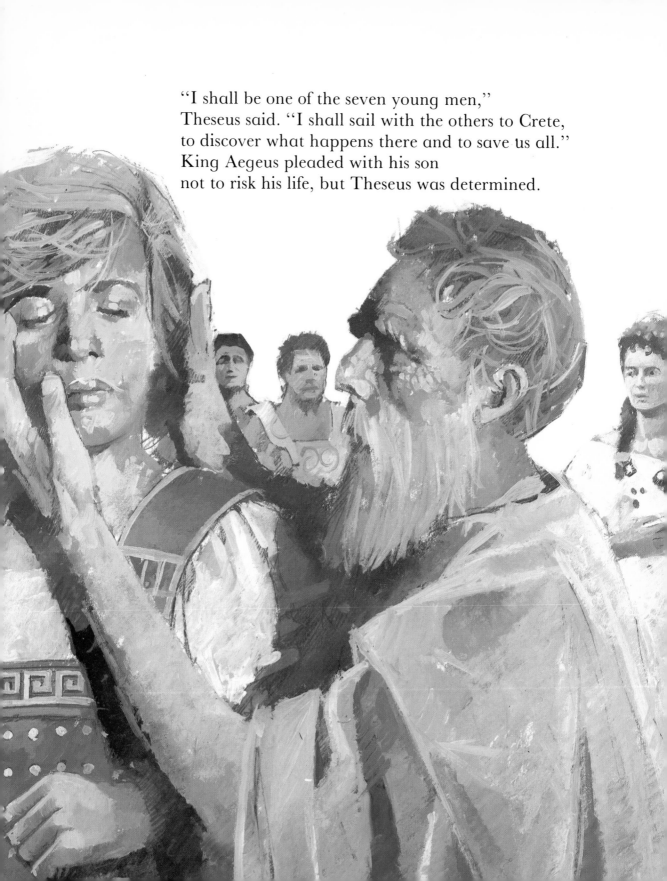

"I shall be one of the seven young men,"
Theseus said. "I shall sail with the others to Crete,
to discover what happens there and to save us all."
King Aegeus pleaded with his son
not to risk his life, but Theseus was determined.

He promised that if he came back safely
his ship should carry white sails.
If he died in Crete,
his sailors should hoist sails of black.

Two DAYS LATER, HE AND THE OTHER YOUNG MEN AND WOMEN
embarked in the long black ship
to sail for Crete,
while the mothers and fathers left behind
mourned and wept for their children.

As they sailed across the dark sea to Crete,
Theseus and the other boys
practised their skill in fighting.
They taught the girls how to fight, too.
Theseus made two of the boys curl their hair
and wear women's long skirts, so that when they arrived
the girls would have two experienced fighters with them.

On the harbour-side in Crete
a great crowd was waiting to greet them;
soldiers, and nobles and ladies of the court.
King Minos was there himself
to make sure that all the young Athenians were there.

Minos did not know that one of the boys
was Theseus, the young prince of Athens.
He heard Theseus say,
"Poseidon, the god of the sea, will protect me."
This angered Minos. He took off his signet ring
and threw it into the sea.
"May Poseidon help you to find that," he cried.

At once, Theseus dived into the sea,
where Poseidon sent a school of dolphins
to guide him to the palace of the mermaids.
The mermaid queen
gave Theseus a crown of jewels
and showed him where Minos' ring had fallen.

When Theseus returned from the sea-bed,
Minos commanded his soldiers
to take the seven boys and seven girls
to his palace.
"Guard them well for tonight," he said.
"Tomorrow they will need no guard
for tomorrow they will die."
Minos and his courtiers went back to the palace,
and the soldiers followed with their prisoners.

As the young Athenians were taken into the palace,
Ariadne, Minos' daughter,
saw Theseus among the boys bound with ropes.
He was handsome and strong and in that moment,
she fell in love with him.

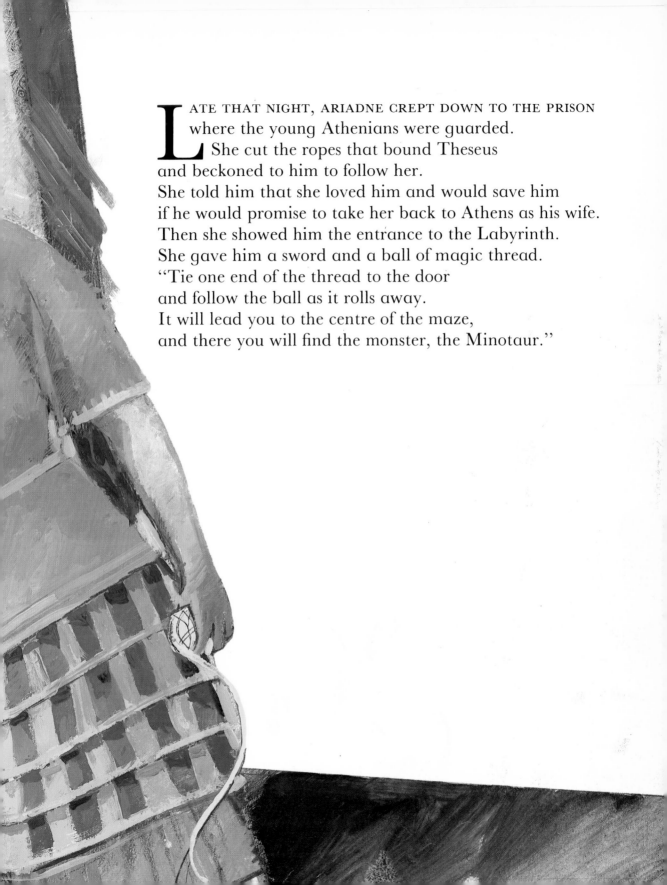

LATE THAT NIGHT, ARIADNE CREPT DOWN TO THE PRISON
where the young Athenians were guarded.
She cut the ropes that bound Theseus
and beckoned to him to follow her.
She told him that she loved him and would save him
if he would promise to take her back to Athens as his wife.
Then she showed him the entrance to the Labyrinth.
She gave him a sword and a ball of magic thread.
"Tie one end of the thread to the door
and follow the ball as it rolls away.
It will lead you to the centre of the maze,
and there you will find the monster, the Minotaur."

THESEUS TIED THE MAGIC THREAD
to the door,
and he followed the ball
as it rolled away from him,
through the twisting passages of the great maze.
In the darkness, he kept his hand on the thread,
and soon he heard a horrible sound.
It was the roar of a savage animal,
but it was also the voice of a man in pain
and despair.

The sound became louder and nearer.
Now Theseus saw the glimmer of light ahead.
He knew that he must be approaching
the centre of the Labyrinth,
the home of the monster, the Minotaur.
Theseus' hand tightened on his sword.
A terrible shadow fell across him.

Theseus stepped forward.
He found himself in a huge cavern,
lit by torches,
and there he saw the great creature,
half man, half bull,
stamping on the stone floor in a blind rage;
desperate, hated, feared, alone.

There was no time for Theseus to stare
in horror and shock.
The Minotaur hurled itself across the floor
to gore him to death with its cruel horns.
Theseus leapt aside
and as the monster crashed past him,
he lunged with the sword,
then struck again and again,
until the wounded creature fell to the ground,
and lay dead among the bones of his victims.

THEN THESEUS LEFT THAT PLACE OF DEATH
and followed the magic thread back
through the web of passages
to the entrance where Ariadne waited for him.
When she saw Theseus return, alive and well,
with the blood of the Minotaur on his sword,
she embraced him and was glad.

TOGETHER ARIADNE AND THESEUS
went to the prison
to find the other young Athenians.
Theseus cut the ropes that bound them
and when they were free, they killed their guards
and escaped from the palace.
They stole out of the palace of Knossos
and went down to the harbour.

There they embarked on the ship which had brought them,
and sailed away, back to safety in Athens.

But Theseus forgot his promise to his father.
King Aegeus was watching for the ship from a high rock.
He saw the black sails and thought his son was dead.
In despair, he threw himself down into the sea.